T0380834

MY GIFT TO YOU

"PROPHETICPOETRY"

SEQUEL

TONIDA JACQUELINE COOPER

To order additional copies of this book, contact:
Xlibris
1-888-795-4274
www.Xlibris.com
Orders@Xlibris.com

ISBN: Softcover   978-1-4535-7801-8
         EBook   978-1-7960-4731-8

Print information available on the last page

Rev. date: 08/16/2019

INTRODUCTION

I want to praise Yahuah for finishing this Sequel, My Gift to You, in a timely fashion. Just released the first one and finished the second one in time for readers to possibly purchase both at the same time. The Sequel is catered more towards couples that are either courting or are already married. The rest are "words of wisdom" to encourage individuals that have faced very hard circumstances in life.

Coming Soon...

Secular Songs That Effect the Spirit Positively or Negatively

PREFACE

I am so grateful that my daughter is home from college to proofread this for me. She saved me money in publishing because of it. Thank you lady "J" (better known as Jazz), of course I cannot thank my Shamayim (heavenly father) enough for this blessing. I have been working on these books for years but it was one thing or another that kept me from finishing them. However, now is the time for it to be exposed, everything is done in Yah's time.

CHAPTER I

FALLING IN LOVE AGAIN

AT THE NICK OF TIME

At the nick of time
You were sent to me
In the midst of Yah's
Healing

The last finishing touch
Yah allowed it to be
through you

You became
the melting of my Ice
cubes

Now I have no reason
To feud………..

I'm now on another flight
because your love helped
to tame my plight……….

At the nick of time you
were heaven sent

This poem developed from a relationship with a person that I thought I would be with for the rest of my life. However, he did not want to step forward and be a responsible man so I had to end it. As far as intellectual conversation, we had a lot in common when it came to the things of Yahuah. We both met those qualifications but the only difference is that I was willing to go forth to the next step but he was afraid to step out of his comfort zone and I realized that he was not as mature as I thought so that was that.

"THEN CAME YOU"

Thought I was doomed
Was no longer groomed
For being me

Really confused didn't
know what to do

THEN CAME YOU

Abused and misunderstood,
did things I never thought
I could

THEN CAME YOU

While being under a pagan religion that almost destroyed
me
 and everything I once believed turned out to be lies.

I became depressed and wanted to die because
I thought that there was no more hope inside,

Although I examined the scriptures like
a fine tooth comb but still ended up confused,

Thought the rest of my life would
Be totally blue

THEN CAME YOU

This poem was written during the time I had came into the true knowledge of finding out that my true heritage is that of a Hebrew Yisrealite. I met this man that is much more knowledgeable in the truth and I learned a lot from him. What he taught me helped me to understand and had taken away the confusion, but some things that I learned are still depressing to know because I had believed a lie for so long and it's said to say but it seemed much simpler and comforting. Maybe if I had been taught the truth from the beginning it would have not taken such an impact on me.

TWO HEARTS THAT BECAME ONE

TWO HEARTS ONCE BROKEN TO PIECES,
BECAME ONE

THEY EACH SAUGHT A COMPANION THAT FIT
THEIR PROFILE BUT COULD FIND NONE,

OF COURSE THEY MET COUNTERFEITS THAT
PLAY THAT ROLE, BUT PRETENTION WAS FOUND
TO BE THE TRUTH ABOUT THEM, SO IT ONLY LAST
A LITTLE WHILE,

IT DIDN'T TAKE LONG TO SEE
RIGHT THROUGH, BECAUSE THEY
SOON REALIZED THAT THE
COUNTERFIET WAS NOT THEIR
STYLE

THEN ONE DAY YAH SAW
FIT TO HAVE THEM MEET

BOTH SEASONED AND FULL OF
UNCONDITIONAL LOVE,
COMPASSION, ROMANCE,
ENCOURAGEMENT AND
SUPPORT

THEY KNEW RIGHT FROM THE START THAT THEY BELONGED TO ONE ANOTHER
THEIR GIFTS OF WRITING GIVEN BY YAH MINISTERED TO EACH OTHER
THEY WERE ALREADY ONE IN THE SPIRIT BECAUSE YAH PUT THEM TOGETHER

A TRUE MAN AND WOMAN OF YAH THAT LIVE APART
IN SEPARATE STATES THAT STILL BECAME ONE
BECAUSE OF YAH, NOT FATE
THEY HAVE NO NEED OF SPOIL (to lose valuable or useful qualities usually as a result of decay)
BECAUSE THEY TRUST IN EACH OTHER THROUGH YAH

MY MAN'S HANDS

YOU SAY YOUR HANDS ARE ROUGH AS SAND,

AND THAT THEY'RE NOT WORTHY TO TOUCH
OR TO SHAKE MY HAND,

BUT I KNOW YOU ARE A HARD WORKING MAN,
A MAN THAT DOES NOT MIND GETTING
YOUR HANDS DIRTY,

JUST LIKE A SOFT FLOWER CENTERED AND,
SECURED IN THE PALM OF YOUR HANDS,

THAT'S HOW I FEEL FROM YOUR GENTLE TOUCH,
WHEN YOU TAKE ME IN YOUR ARMS
AND HOLD MY HAND

THE BEAUTY OF YOU MY MAN
IS THAT YOU'RE GENTLE EVEN
WHEN YOUR HANDS FEEL A LITTLE ROUGH,

AND BECAUSE THEY ARE MY MAN HANDS,
FOR ME THAT'S GOOD ENOUGH

This poem derived from a conversation I held with a gentleman I use to work with. He was so funny. He and I always talked about getting pampered, he through his wife, and I through the salon, getting manicures and pedicures. Well, this guy also did landscape work on the side. And he always use to shake my hand but this particular day he had just finished some landscaping work and decided that his hands felt like sand and were unworthy to shake my hand, and that is where this poem developed, along with a little imagination with my own man hands.

MARRIAGE COVENANT

ON THIS DAY, WE COME TOGETHER IN MATRIMONY,
BEFORE YAHUAH WITH HIS APPROVAL, BEFORE

GUESTS, FAMILY, AND FRIENDS, AS A WITNESS TO US BECOMING ONE,
WE SHALL JOURNEY THROUGH

THE YEARS OF OUR LIFE TOGETHER,
I HAVE NO FEAR THAT SOME DAY THIS MARRIAGE WILL
DEPART BECAUSE I KNEW YOU WERE MY HUSBAND RIGHT FROM THE START,

I'VE WAITED PATIENTLY FOR YOU TO APPEAR IN MY LIFE;
YAHUAH HAS CUSTOM MADE US FOR ONE ANOTHER,
WE ARE DESIGNER ORIGINALS STRAIGHT FROM YAH,

YAHUAH TOLD ME THAT MY HUSBAND WILL BE A YAH FEARING MAN
WITH MUCH LOVE, PATIENCE AND UNDERSTANDING,
HE WILL LOVE ME LIKE YAHUSHUA LOVES THE BODY OF THE HEBREW YISREALITES

I'M THAT YAH FEARING WOMAN WHOM YAH HAS SENT YOU,
I WILL BE SUBMISSIVE TO YOU,

LOVE YOU UNCONDITIONALLY AND SUPPORT YOUR YAH GIVEN DECISIONS,
I KNOW WHEN PEOPLE GET MARRIED THEY DON'T THINK ABOUT THE TURMOIL AHEAD

AND IT'S FOOLISH AND NAIVE TO THINK THAT IT WILL BE PERFECT,
MAYBE NEXT TO, BUT NOT PERFECT, NOTHING IS PERFECT UNTIL WE REACH ETERNAL LIFE WITH YAH

HOWEVER WE MUST KEEP IN MIND THAT WE CAN DO ALL THINGS
THROUGH YAH THAT STRENGTHENS US,
LET'S KEEP IN MIND THAT WE MUST HONOR ONE ANOTHER,

LET'S KEEP IN MIND THAT OUR BODIES NO LONGER BELONG TO US AS INDIVIDUALS
BUT TO ONE ANOTHER, LET'S KEEP IN MIND TO NOT LET THE SUN GO DOWN ON OUR WRATH,

LET'S KEEP IN MIND TO GET DOWN ON OUR KNEES TOGETHER AND PRAY,
LET'S KEEP IN MIND TO GO TO YAHUAH INDIVIDUALLY,
AS WELL AS ON A DAILY BASIS FOR ONE ANOTHER,
LET'S KEEP IN MIND THAT ALL THINGS WORK TOGETHER FOR THE GOOD
OF THOSE THAT LOVE YAH THAT ARE CALLED ACCORDING TO HIS PURPOSE,

LET'S KEEP IN MIND THAT NOT ONLY DID YAHUAH BRING US TOGETHER FOR EACH OTHER,
BUT ALSO FOR HIS KINGDOM, BECAUSE YOUR GIFTS AND CALL
AND MY GIFTS AND CALL COMPLIMENTS EACH OTHER

IT'S POWERFUL, LIFE CHANGING, AND LIFE SAVING,
I NEVER KNEW THAT IT WAS HUMANLY POSSIBLE FOR SOMEONE TO LOVE
ME LIKE YOU DO, I LOVE YOU TOO,
I CHERISH YOU, AND I'M SO GLAD YAHUAH SENT YOU,

WE ARE THAT MARRIAGE WITH AN EVER LASTING SPARK
EVEN AS WE GET OLD AND WRINKLE WE'LL STILL HAVE THAT FIRE AND DESIRE FOR EACH OTHER,
PEOPLE WILL LOOK AT OUR MARRIAGE AND KNOW THAT IT IS POSSIBLE TO
HAVE A JOYOUS MARRIAGE, EVEN IN THIS CORRUPT SOCIETY
BECAUSE WHEN WE OBEY YAHUAH, HIS PERFECT WILL FOR US IS ACCOMPLISHED,

TO OUR MARRIAGE MADE IN SHAMAYIM (HEAVEN), OUR COMMITMENT AND DEVOTION
ON THIS DAY, I VOW TO BE WITH YOU FOREVER, TILL DEATH DO US PART "SO BE IT"

YOUR OBEDIENT WIFE

Being your obedient wife
has been the best thing
in my life since Yah snatched
me out of my sin and gave me life
again

It is a pleasure to cater to you
your every need, that I want to
exceed.

My every awakened thought
is to know how I will please my
husband day by day,

I want to constantly please
you in every way

When we make love I totally
lose myself in you,
I guess it has something to do
with being chosen for you

You are the covenant of our
family.

I trust that you will take care
of us because in Yah I know
you trust

I love you my darling to the
end of time through hard
times, peace, and world crime

AFTER THE FIRST TIME IT ONLY GETS BETTER

After waiting and saving yourself for so long
to be with that brand knew spouse,
Learning the pleasures of each other's
needs and wants only gets better
Exploring each other's body and finding
things that you never knew is part of the
excitement in the honeymoon
Intimate moments that are shared together
is more than penetration and an orgasm
It is the very essence of becoming one
 spirit by transition of intellect
and emotions,
Once the climax is reached then
it's time for cuddling, whispered
conversations, telling each other
 "I love you" and before you
know it, your making love again.
Through the thoughts and
physical body, the second
time was better than the
first and so on, because
 the cycle repeats itself
 by getting better and
better.

I chose this background because this poem is about a husband and a wife
making love. The two of them are in such harmony with one another that
the violin is one of the best instruments that I could think of that fits this
description in their love making.

MY HUSBAND OF WISDOM

When I'm with my husband that's full of wisdom
I feel so secure.......

When it comes to a question,
I know through my husband
and Yah I can be sure...

I love the idea of taking on his last
name....

That means more to me than being in a hall of fame

He makes me feel like I'm the only woman
In the world.............

Treating me with caution, because to him
I'm more precious than a pearl............

Everyday and night we go to
higher heights............

Expressing our love to each other
soft as a cloud..............

When we make love we give
each other a crown.............

It is simply a reminder that when
Yah puts two people together

Nothing can separate us, even as
This world is turned upside down..............

This poem came to me when I imagined the ideal husband to have. To honor me, protect me and love me unconditionally. Many women have a problem with being obedient to their husbands, but in my opinion any woman who is treated as this poem says should have no problems with being submissive, I know I wouldn't. Now don't get me wrong, I do know that if a man is not treating his wife with honor and respect and he's being abusive to her, that is not the behavior to be submissive to. However when he honor her and loves her like Yahushua loves the body of the Messiah then there should be no problem with submission.

HUSBAND & WIFE DAY

OH HOW NICE IT WOULD BE
TO MARK THE CALENDAR TO SET ASIDE
AN INTERNATIONAL DAY OF CELEBRATION,
CALLING IT HUSBAND & WIFE DAY

THE WORLD CELEBRATE BIRTHDAYS
AND HOLIDAYS OF ALL SORTS

EVEN PUT A DAY ASIDE FOR SOME
SPORTS LIKE "THE SUPER BOWL"

WHY NOT HAVE A REMINDER
OF HOW IMPORTANT MARRIAGE
PLAYS IN THE ROLE OF BEING ONE

SHATAN (DEVIL) HAS USED PEOPLE
TO DOWN PLAY MARRIAGE
AND TURNED MANY HEADS INTO
THINKING THAT MARRIAGE IS DEAD

ALL OF HIS CUNNING TRICKS AND TRADES
IS TO TELL THE WORLD THAT THE THING TO DO
IS TO HAVE MULTIPLE PARTNERS WHILE
TAKING THE RISK OF DEVELOPING AIDS

YOU SEE SEX IS GREAT WHEN YOUR SPOUSE IS
YOUR MATE,

CASUAL SEX WILL MAKE ONE SPIRIT VEXED,
BECAUSE MARRIAGE IS HONORABLE AND
THE BED IS NOT TO BE DEFILED.

NOT ONLY THAT BUT ONE IS NEVER
FULFILLED BECAUSE THERE IS A HIGH PRICE
TO PAY FOR A CASUAL LAY.

WITH EVERY PARTNER YOU HAVE
ENCOUNTERED, YOU'VE SLEPT WITH EVERY PARTNER
THEY HAVE ENCOUNTERED

LET'S UP LIFT MARRIAGE AND PUT SEX BACK IN PERSPECTIVE,
THE WAY YAH CREATED IT TO BE. TO BE WED IN ORDER FOR
MAN & WOMAN TO ENTER THE BED

To set aside a day for something is supposed to be of importance and recognized worldwide if possible. This world has gotten away from the importance of marriage. I think that it would be nice to set aside a day internationally in celebration. Without saying, of course couples should express this all the time but having a day set aside would be nice too.

GOLDEN WEDDING ANNIVERSARY

WHO WOULD EVER THINK A LOVELY COUPLE
LIKE YOU

WOULD BECOME ONE OF THE GREATEST
AMONG THE FEW

WHEN THE TWO OF YOU FIRST MET
IT SEEMED TO BE SUGAR AND SALT
BUT AFTER A FEW CONVERSATIONS

YOU TWO BECAME THE ULTIMATE MALT,
IN OTHER WORDS THE COUPLE THAT CLUSTERED

IT IS NOT OFTEN THAT PEOPLE TODAY
MAKE IT TO THEIR GOLDEN ANNIVERSARY DATE

THROUGHOUT THE YEARS OF TRIAL AND ERROR

YOU REFUSED TO LET YOUR MARRIAGE
TURN INTO TERROR

AND BECAUSE OF THAT
YOU HAVE STOOD THE TEST OF ALL
THROUGH THE GOOD TIMES AND THE
BAD TIMES

SO IN ABSOLUTE HONOR TO YOU,
FROM YOUR FAMILY AND FRIENDS TOO,
OUR PRAYERS ARE WITH YOU….
THAT YOU CONTINUE TO DO WHAT YOU
DO

TO KEEP YOUR MARRIAGE FROM FALLING APART
AND ENJOY AS ONE, TIL DEATH DO YOU PART.

BOTH, MARRIED COUPLES AND POTENTIAL MARRIED
COUPLES ADORE YOU AND HAVE HOPES TO HAVE
A GREAT MARRIAGE LIKE YOU DO

This poem was originally written for a couple that reached their golden
anniversary. I thought that it would be nice to add to this section to em-
phasize how important marriage is and how married couples rarely reach
their golden anniversary today.

CHAPTER II

WORDS OF WISDOM

"Our Creator's Name"
What Happened TO IT?

VIGOROUS WITH LIES DISPLAYED AS TRUTH,
WHEN WILL YOU COME TO TRUCE?

THOSE THAT CALL THEMSELVES CHILDREN
OF OUR CREATOR

HOW CAN YOU SAY YOU LOVE HIM WHEN
YOU DON'T RESPECT HIS NAME?

HOW DO YOU EXPECT FOR HIM TO
PROTECT YOU WHEN YOU CALL
THE WRONG NAME?

NOT TO BE CARNAL, BUT TO CALL OUT
ANOTHER'S NAME MISTAKENED FOR HIS,
IS LIKE A MAN MAKING LOVE TO HIS WIFE
AND SHE CALLS OUTANOTHER MAN'S NAME

JUST LIKE PARENTS GIVING THEIR
NEWBORN CHILD A MEANINGFUL NAME,
BUT THE CHILD DOESN'T LIKE IT
BECAUSE IT IS NOT POPULAR,

HE/SHE GROWS UP, CHANGE THE NAME,
BREAK THEIR PARENTS HEART AND
PUT THEM TO SHAME

TO NOT RESPECT OUR CREATOR'S NAME,
I BELIEVE HE FEELS THE SAME

THOSE THAT DIDN'T KNOW ANY BETTER YAH
EXCUSED YOU, BUT NOW THAT YOU KNOW THE TRUTH,
WHAT WILL YOU DO?

HOW IS IT THAT YOU FIND OUT THE TRUTH ABOUT THESE
PAGAN NAMES, REFUSE TO TURN AND REPENT, BUT DETERMINED
TO CALL ON NAMES OF GOD, LORD AND JESUS THAT ARE IN VAIN?

THOSE NAMES HAVE NOTHING TO DO WITH OUR CREATOR AND HIS
PRESCIOUS SON'S NAME, YAHUAH OUR CREATOR AND YAHSHUA HIS SON

BOTH ARE POWERFUL NAMES ABOVE ALL, FATHER YAHUAH IS MERCIFUL
AND FULL OF EXTENEDED FAVOR THAT HE OFTEN SENDS

BUT ONCE THE TRUTH IS REVEALED THERE IS NO MORE SACRIFICE
OF SINS (Hebrew 10:26)

I LOVE YOU YAHUAH THROUGH YOUR SON YAHUSHUA WHO DIED
FOR ME ON GOLGOTHA, NAILED TO A STAKE SO THAT I CAN ESCAPE
THE HORRORS OF THE PAGAN MESS OF THE UNITED STATES

This poem was written when I first started learning about the real name of the creator.

CHOSEN BY YAHUAH TO SPEAK THE TRUTH

CHOSEN TO SPEAK THE TRUTH BUT WHEN THE CHALLENGE
COMES, DID HE PASS THE TEST OR DID IT SHOW
THE REVELATION OF HIS TRUE QUEST

I LEARNED THAT A MAN THAT REALLY LOVES HIS MAKER
AND IS TOUCHED BY YAH TO SPEAK, HE MUST ALSO PRAY
THAT FATHER REMOVES THE WORLDLY DESIRE OF WHAT
HIS FLESH REALLY WANTS

IT'S SO EASY FOR A MAN TO SAY THAT HE IS NOT PRESSED
WITH A WOMAN THE WORLD CONSIDERS "FINE", BECAUSE
IF SHE DOESN'T HAVE THE SPIRIT OF YAH OR MORALS AND
VALUES OF A WIFE FIT FOR THE MAN OF YAH TO BE WITH FOR
LIFE THAN SHE'S NOT WORTH A DIME

THESE ARE THE THINGS TO SAY BECAUSE HE KNOWS THAT IS
THE RIGHT PATHWAY

AS IF THAT IS REALLY GOOD ENOUGH, HOWEVER IF SHE DOESN'T
HAVE THE SHAPELY TIGHT LEGS AND THE RIGHT SIZE BUTT, PLUS
THE BUST, AS WELL AS THE CUTE OR PRETTY FACE WITH A SMALL
WAIST, DEEP DOWN INSIDE HE IS NOT SATISFIED.

LIVING IN A WORLD SO CRUEL

LIVING IN A WORLD SO CRUEL, FULL OF FOOLS (Psalm 12:1)

WITH MUCH SHAME, PEOPLE PUSHING BLAME,
IGNORANT WITH PRIDE, WON'T SET THE EGO ASIDE

MEN LAME WITH THIS THING THEY CALL GAME,
 MOTHER'S TRYING TO DO IT ALL,
WITH NO HUSBAND TO CATCH THEM IF THEY FALL

MUCH VIOLENCE THROUGHOUT THE WORLD

TERRORIST ON THE RISE AND HAVE BECOME NEIGHBORS
THAT WE DON'T EVEN KNOW UNTIL THEY MAKE THAT BOMB AND
LOSE INNOCENT PEOPLE TO THE BLOW

MOST POLITICANS WITH THEIR CROOKED SELVES, MAKING DECISIONS
THAT TAKES FOOD OFF POOR PEOPLES SHELVES…….

THE HYPE HAS BEEN FOR YEARS TO GET AN EDUCATION,
AND PERSUE A DEGREE, BUT AS I LOOK AROUND TODAY……….
MANY THAT HOLD THAT PIECE OF PAPER HAVE NO FOOD OR NO SHELTER;

I DON'T HAVE ANYTHING AGAINST EDUCATION BUT MY THOUGHTS ARE…..
WHAT IS THE POINT IF YOU PURSUE A DEGREE TO BE
 "EFFECTIVELY COMPETITIVE" AS THEY SAY…..

WHEN MANY CAN'T EVEN FIND A JOB TO AFFORD A PLACE
TO STAY

LIVING IN AMERICA IS SUPPOSE TO BE "THE LAND OF OPPORTUNITY",
BUT HOW QUICKLY THIS IS DECEASING OBVIOUSLY

WITH THE DOWNFALL OF THE ECONOMY STEADILY INCREASING
BECAUSE THERE IS NO MORE MONEY TO CIRCULATE. I'M ALMOST
CERTAIN MUCH OF IT HAS TO DO WITH HIDDEN WATERGATE,

KNEE DEEP IN DEPTH TO FOREIGN COUNTRIES FOR BORROWING
MONEY; SO THIS MEANS THE UNITED NATIONS ARE SERVANTS TO THE
FOREIGN LENDERS…….NOW THAT THE NATIONS IN SUCH A HINDER

THE BORROWER IS A SERVANT TO HIS LENDER (Proverbs 22:7),
AND THE RICH RULE OVER THE POOR.

Hmmm…… KIND OF MAKES YOU WONDER HOW AMERICANS ARE
SERVANTS TO THEM, WILL IT COME TO A POINT WHERE IT WILL
COST AMERICANS TO LOSE THEIR LIMBS?

PEOPLE WE ARE LIVING IN A WORLD WHERE NOTHING IS GURANTEED SO WE NEED TO TAKE HEED
TO THE WARNINGS AND SIGNS OF THE END TIMES THAT SCRIPTURE SPEAKS ABOUT….THE WARS AND
RUMORS OF WARS, FOR NATIONS SHALL RISE AGAINST NATIONS

THE LIGHT IN YOU

The light in you is a reflection of me
through trials, tribulations and persecutions.
The strong tower that I am, you are, because
I live inside of you, and I operate in you

As you abide in me, and my Torah
abides in you, nothing that comes
against you can prosper….

Because I was persecuted
it will happen to you too,

Remember my children, they hated
me first before you and you are in the world
but not of it, the world only accepts their own and if
you were one of them they would accept you too,
so that's why they reject you.

A light house shines over the dark seas, to
give light for the sailors to be able to see.

All kinds of boats, many shapes and sizes are
able to pass through because of this light.

Same as you my children; the light that shines
within you gives light to this dark cold world,

People from all walks of life will see,
and be drawn to you because of me, that
lives in you; they are able to pass through the evil
that this world have to offer

The light in you is my torah that shines
it's a reflection of me that draws
the lost,

I love you my child and remember I will never leave you nor forsake you,
I am with you always to the end.

This poem was written through the inspiration that I have in Yahuah

A MAN OF HUMBLENESS

A Man of Honor, a man of love…..
A man of sensitivity, a man of
productivity in everything that you do

Such a gentleman, not full of pride,
Once I got to know you I knew someday
I'd be your bride.

A man that can admit when you're wrong………

This certainly shows that your strength
is "Strong"

No ego trips, you're so loving,
that your hard knocks of life never
developed strife

Instead you have grown to a maturity
whatever Yah says it's done.

So giving, not expecting nothing in return

You lived a life of struggle and pain, by being broken through life, but you learned that the cares of this life will burn, so now the things that you yearn are the things of Yah, because you know in every part of your life in Yah you must turn

MAN I MET IN YAH LEFT SUCH AN IMPRESSION ABOUT HIM THAT I WROTE THIS POEM ABOUT HIS CHARACTER.

A BABY BOY

A baby boy turns into a preschooler,
then transforms to a little boy that becomes a teen
then a man.

During these precious times of change,
a baby boy needs to be protected, nurtured,
and loved unconditionally.

A boy needs to experience his mother's soft touch and gentleness
this will help him to turn into a **_gentleman_** that his wife will
appreciate

His father's protection and guidance will make him balance
 to know how to face a challenge in life like a man should,
and not run from it.

This is why he needs to be guided by love and nurture,
he must be balanced with discipline and love.

A baby boy needs to be taught that being tough doesn't
make him a man, but using his mind and building his
character through courage and integrity, shapes him into a man.

Last but not least, when the baby boy becomes a young man
he needs to be taught how to treat young ladies like a lady,
shivery will not die. If he is taught to find interest in
a young lady intellectually, beyond the physical, which many
times inspire promiscuous activity he will learn to respect his temple
 and hers too, until he meets the right lady that carries herself like
a princess that also respects her temple

**In my opinion this poem was written to say this is one of the healthiest ways in rais-
ing a baby boy.**

A BABYGIRL

A baby girl is precious as a pearl,
gentle as a flower and delicate as powder.

Pretty in pink and looks like a baby doll when sleep,
she needs the touch and security from both mother and father,
to know she is secured for keeps.

A baby girl turns into a preschooler while wearing
pony tails and dainty dresses,

Then turns into a little girl,
where she is then transformed into a teenager,
to become a young lady. Developed physically,
while vulnerable to the influence of
her environment.

Therefore she needs her mother to teach her how
to carry herself like a lady, and respect herself
as well as demand respect. To teach her not to
be a man chaser but men are suppose
to be the aggressor and the pursuer

She needs her mom to help teach her little things, like clean hygiene,
to be primp and to care for others, not to be selfish. To not envy what another girl have, but
work with what she has, because she is her own unique beautiful self , and she must love
herself and don't look for validation from others.

She needs her mother to tell her that it's is ok to be educated, work,
be a wife and a mom too, but to make sure the man she accepts as a spouse
she can submit to, so chose wisely

A little girl needs her father to tell her that she is
his little princess and that he will be there to protect her
and to make her feel secure and significant

To tell her that he loves her and compliments her while being her
cheerleader, as well as encourage her potential gifts and talents.

As she continues to grow as a teenager she needs the balance of both
parents to prepare her for this cold cruel world.

She needs her daddy to reinforce to her that she is beautiful,
he will protect her, make her feel secured and loved by him.

A young lady needs her father to hug her and show her affection,
to listen and be there in her most defenseless times to reassure her
that everything will be alright, so when she becomes a young woman
she will not be looking for affection and significance in a man that
may take her for granted.

**THIS POEM WAS WRITTEN IN REGARDS TO HOW MUCH LITTLE GIRLS NEED WELL
ROUNDED TENDER LOVE AND CARE.**

"MEN LET YAH BE YOUR SPOUSE"

IT MAY BE STRANGE FOR A MAN
OF YAH TO LOOK AT YAH AS A SPOUSE

BUT IN REALITY, YAH SAID THAT HE
WILL BE EVERYTHING THAT WE NEED
FOR HIM TO BE, THEREFORE MEN
GO BEFORE HIM AND DON'T FLEE

JUST AS A EARLTHLY WOMAN IS TO HER HUSBAND
AS A HELP MEET………

MEN YAH WILL BE THE SAME FOR YOU

YAH WILL MEET YOU IN YOUR
MOST TROUBLESOME TIMES IF YOU LET HIM

HE WILL MEET YOU WHERE YOU
WERE BROKEN AND DARKNESS WAS SPOKEN

LIKE A FIRE ON A TORCH
HE WILL SPEAK LIFE SO YOUR
SPIRIT WILL REUNITE

DON'T BE AFRAID TO CRY OUT TO HIM
COME TO HIM NAKED, OPEN AND HONESTLY, AND
LET HIM CLOTH YOU

LET THE TEARS FALL DOWN YOUR FACE,
DON'T YOU DARE THINK THAT A MAN
IS NOT SUPPOSE TO CRY LIKE THE
WORLD TEACHES

THIS IS WHY SO MANY MEN ARE NOT
WALKING WHAT THEY PREACH

THEY ARE AFRAID TO ADMIT THAT THEY FAILED
BECAUSE THEY DID NOT CONSULT WITH YAH
BEFORE MAKING A DECESION………
NOW IT SEEMS THEIR LIFE IS A COLLISION

IT IS OK TO ADMIT THAT YOU WERE WRONG
CONFESS, REPENT AND START A FRESH AND
NEW WITH HIM SO THAT HE CAN MINISTER
TO YOU, JUST AS A WIFE SUPPORTS HER HUSBAND

MOST OF ALL, READ HIS TORAH AND SPEAK IT OVER
YOURSELF, FOR THIS IS THE LIFE THAT HE CREATED
FOR YOU; TO HAVE HIS LOVE IN WHICH YOU WILL
NOT FAIL TO MATURITY IN THE SPIRIT, SO CONTINUE
TO SEEK HIS FACE AND LET HIM DIRECT YOUR TRAIL……………

CONCEPTION IS LIFE UNLESS YOU KILL IT

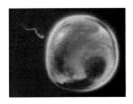

JAN 1

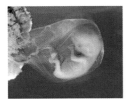

Feb 15

March 6

March 8

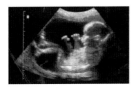

March 12

Today I am conceived through my mommy & daddy. They don't know it yet, but I have just begun the developing stages of their DNA which determines the traits and features of my loving parents. I am so excited that I can't wait to meet them, and I know they will be even more excited to find out about me too.

I am now forming a body with all of my limbs and skin, finger nails and hair. I know mommy will be happy to see that I have her caramel brown skin and my father will be overjoyed to see that I have big brown eyes like him. Oh how I can't wait for them to see their baby girl. I look forward to being cuddled in my parent's arms, getting warm baths and many hugs. I feel so protected by them already.

Mommy is feeling sick now and she thinks that she has a flu virus, so she made an appointment to go to the doctor's. Oh how surprised she will be to find out that she does not have a sickly virus but instead a beautiful little girl growing inside of her every day. I am so excited to have a mommy and daddy that will love me and protect me, to play with me in a game of peek-a-boo and Eskimo noses, and most of all to see them glow when I say mommy and daddy for the first time. Oh boy! The fun it will be to crawl and take my first steps, fall down and get up as my mommy and daddy hold out their loving arms as I walk towards them. As I try not to fall they will cheer me on, but if I do, then I will get up and try again and make it to their arms to be hugged. I just love my mommy and daddy so much and I know they love me twice as much because I belong to them their own flesh and blood.

This is the day my mommy goes to the doctor's to find out that I am conceived. She will be real happy when the Doctor gives her the good news about me. Yes, Yes, mommy is about to find out about me. The examination began and the testing has taken place. The results are in and the Doctor is telling my mommy now. I just know she is so happy that she can't wait to tell my daddy. I wish I could see their faces as they share in the good news of my delivery in six months.

Mommy is now calling the office to make another appointment to go to the doctors. I'm thinking that it is to start her prenatal care so that I am really healthy when I arrive. I can imagine that mommy and daddy are having lots of fun preparing for me to come by announcing their good news, and thinking of names for me according to my gender. I know I will love my nursery that they are preparing for me. I am so excited I can't wait to be gently laid in my beautiful plush crib that mommy and daddy prepared for me.

Today is extraordinary because this is the day mommy and daddy both go to the Doctor's together. Hurray! they must be so excited about me like I thought they would because they are in this step by step together. I think they have just arrived at the doctor's to be seen. Now she and daddy are waiting for the doctor. The nurse is now leading mommy and daddy to the examination room. Mommy is getting up on the hospital bed now.

They are probably preparing mommy for a sonogram so that she and daddy can see my development stage in mommy's belly. Wait, "Oh no! mommy, daddy what's happening?" "This hurts, what is that thing pulling me apart?" "Please help me mommy?" "Daddy save me I thought you loved me?" "Why mommy? Why daddy? Why are you allowing them to do this to me? I love you why won't you let me live? I thought you loved me too.

"I was so excited to see my parents soon but now I vanished, because today is the day my parents killed me, by aborting me.

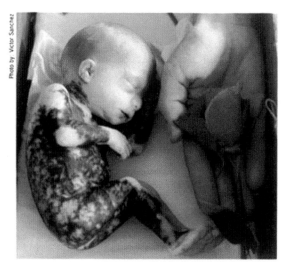

This picture is a snap shot of a baby girl @ 4 ½ months
of development that was burned to death from
the saline solution used to abort her.

Quoted from the picture: "We have been led to believe that
having an abortion is a mass of tissue," look at this little
girl she is more than a mass of tissue, she is a perfectly formed
human being.

I wrote this poem and added the three developing stages to show people that fetuses are more than just tissue, and to show that they have their five senses within the first month, but the average woman doesn't even know that they are pregnant until their 3rd month.

Please see below: This is the process of a Partial Birth Abortion

The Partial Birth Abortion Procedure

 Guided by ultrasound, the abortionist grabs the baby's leg with forceps.

 The baby's leg is pulled out into the birth canal.

 The abortionist delivers the baby's entire body, except for the head.

 The abortionist jams scissors into the baby's skull. The scissors are then opened to enlarge the hole...

 The scissors are removed and a suction catheter is inserted. The child's brains are sucked out, causing the skull to collapse. The dead baby is then removed.

Abortions are steady rising in number. To the women that are considering an abortion, please reconsider and look into putting your baby up for an adoption. Only you know the reason why you want to pass the baby up. I don't know what your situation is or what happened in your life to consider having an abortion. But many would love to raise a brand new infant of their own. I'm not judging you nor am I your creator to do so. You have to answer to Him one day, but writing this poem and submitting this information on abortions are solely to educate. Again the average woman does not know that she is pregnant until the 3rd month of pregnancy. Some people do not know this information to even reconsider their decisions. Also I meant to mention that during the process of abortions the baby does have all five senses. So they can feel the burn of the saline and the cuts from the scissors and blades.

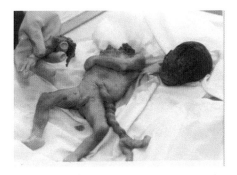

This is a picture of a baby that was aborted through "Partial Birth Abortion"

MOTHER

A MOTHER IS WISE
 SHE KEEPS HOPE ALIVE,

WHEN IT COMES TO HER CHILDREN,
SHE WILL DO WHAT OTHERS WON'T DO,

SHE HAS MANY HIDDEN TALENTS
 THAT ARE UNIQUE AND FEW TO THE AVERAGE PERSON

A MOTHER WILL NURTURE,
SHE'S NOT A CURSER (TO BRING HARM)

A MOTHER IS A PROTECTER, WHEN IT COMES TO
HER CHILDREN NO ONE CAN TOUCH HER.

MOTHER'S WILL DO WHAT'S BEST FOR HER CHILDREN
 EVEN IF IT REQUIRES LESS FOR HER

A MOTHER WILL SACRIFICE,
SHE KNOW IT'S A
POWERFUL DEVICE

YOU KNOW HAVING
A LOVING MOTHER
IS REALLY NICE

**Reminiscing my duties as a mother
is when this poem was inspired**

28

A MAN WITH SUCH POTENTIAL

A MAN WITH SUCH POTENTIAL
SO PERSONAL, BUT YET CONFIDENTIAL

HIS DEMEANOR OF LENDING A HAND
BIG OR SMALL, EACH TIME HE
HELPS, IT MAKES HIM FEEL TALL...............

LIKE MANY OF US HE HAS HIS FLAWS
BUT EACH ONE CREATED HAS A CAUSE.................

HIS HEART IS PURE AS GOLD.
EACH DAY HE GROWS IN YAH
HIS LIFE WILL UNFOLD

TO WHOM HE WAS CHOSEN TO BE,
A CHOSEN VESSLE TO SPEAK........
FOR YAH A TRUE MOUTH PEACE WHEN
IT COMES TO SCRIPTURE

THROUGH YAH THERE IS NO FEAR,
LIKE KING DAVID WHEN HE KILLED THE
GIANT....................

THE TRUE POWER WAS THE FATHER
STANDING BEHIND DAVID, IT REALLY HAD
NOTHING TO DO WITH HIS SLING SHOT.........

THE POWER WAS FROM YAH IN
WHICH HE GOT.................

I SAY THE SAME TO YOU MAN OF YAH,
TO STAND UP AND FIGHT...........

WHILE KNOWING THAT YAH IS THE
CENTER OF YOUR FIGHT...........

SO DON'T FRET THE PLIGHT, HOLD ON
MAN OF YAH AND TRUST IN HIM...........
BECAUSE HE CREATED YOU TO BE LIKE HIM

A MINISTER OF YAH

A MINISTER OF LOVE
A MINISTER THAT KEEPS IT REAL

A MINISTER OF COURAGE
EVEN WHEN DISCOURAGED
A MINISTER THAT CARES
FOR THE FLOCK YAH SENT

A MINISTER THAT KNOWS
WHEN HE DOES SOMETHING WRONG
TO TURN AND REPENT

A MINISTER OF YAH
THAT'S WHO YOU ARE

ANOINTED FROM HEAD TO TOE
AND CAN TEACH THE TORAH
THAT WILL MAKE THE WIND BLOW

This poem derived from an inspiring minister.

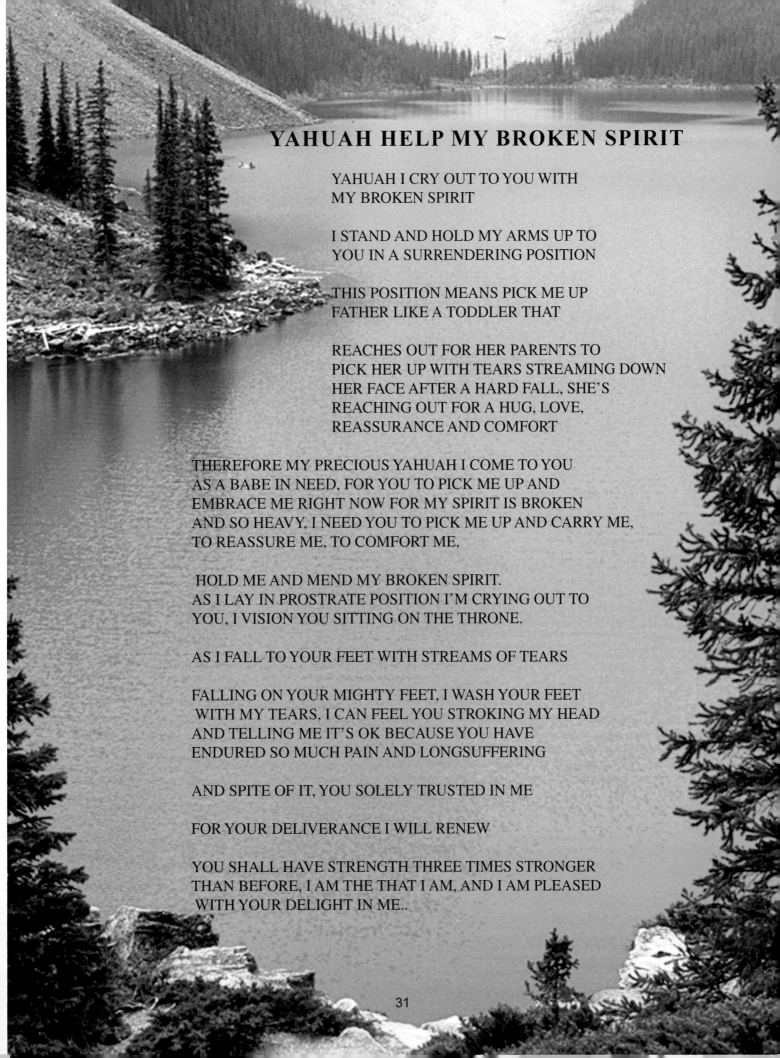

YAHUAH HELP MY BROKEN SPIRIT

YAHUAH I CRY OUT TO YOU WITH
MY BROKEN SPIRIT

I STAND AND HOLD MY ARMS UP TO
YOU IN A SURRENDERING POSITION

THIS POSITION MEANS PICK ME UP
FATHER LIKE A TODDLER THAT

REACHES OUT FOR HER PARENTS TO
PICK HER UP WITH TEARS STREAMING DOWN
HER FACE AFTER A HARD FALL, SHE'S
REACHING OUT FOR A HUG, LOVE,
REASSURANCE AND COMFORT

THEREFORE MY PRECIOUS YAHUAH I COME TO YOU
AS A BABE IN NEED, FOR YOU TO PICK ME UP AND
EMBRACE ME RIGHT NOW FOR MY SPIRIT IS BROKEN
AND SO HEAVY, I NEED YOU TO PICK ME UP AND CARRY ME,
TO REASSURE ME, TO COMFORT ME,

HOLD ME AND MEND MY BROKEN SPIRIT.
AS I LAY IN PROSTRATE POSITION I'M CRYING OUT TO
YOU, I VISION YOU SITTING ON THE THRONE.

AS I FALL TO YOUR FEET WITH STREAMS OF TEARS

FALLING ON YOUR MIGHTY FEET, I WASH YOUR FEET
WITH MY TEARS, I CAN FEEL YOU STROKING MY HEAD
AND TELLING ME IT'S OK BECAUSE YOU HAVE
ENDURED SO MUCH PAIN AND LONGSUFFERING

AND SPITE OF IT, YOU SOLELY TRUSTED IN ME

FOR YOUR DELIVERANCE I WILL RENEW

YOU SHALL HAVE STRENGTH THREE TIMES STRONGER
THAN BEFORE, I AM THE THAT I AM, AND I AM PLEASED
WITH YOUR DELIGHT IN ME..

THE POEM DOCTOR

DR. LEE- DR. LEE
HOW DID THAT NICKNAME
COME TO BE?

FROM YOUR POEMS
WHICH BRINGS HEALING
IN THE MIST OF A STORM

YAHUAH PROVIDED
THIS DAY AND TIME
BEFORE YOU WERE
EVEN BORN

TO HELP OTHERS SEE
THE LIGHT
WHEN THE ENEMY
IS READY TO FIGHT

DR. LEE- DR. LEE
KEEP FIGHTING THE
THE GOOD FIGHT,
AND LET ALL PRAISES
DUE TO YAH
COME TO BE

This poem was inspired because of
a gentleman I met that wrote poetry
too, and he said that people would
tell him that his poetry was healing
for their pain, traumas and psycho-
logical mind set.

CHAPTER III

GENERAL POETRY

SPRING-SPRING

SPRING-SPRING,

JUST DO
YOUR THING,

BLOOM OUT THE

FLOWERS AND
MAKE

THE BIRDS SING

AN AUTUMN DAY

WHAT A DAY, WHAT A DAY, TO RELAX, TO LAY
BACK AND WATCH THE LEAVES FALL,
TO WATCH THE SQUIRRELS HAVE A BALL.....

AS THEY RUN UP AND
DOWN THE TREE,

FEELING FREE, DASHING IN AND OUT OF
THE COLORED LEAVES, OF RED BURGUNDY
AND BLUE, WHILE PLAYING PEAK A BOO,

WITHOUT A CARE IN THE WORLD, HAPPY
BEING SQUIRRELS, DON'T NEED MUCH AT
ALL, BUT NUTS GATHERED AT THE
CAPACITY OF A BARREL,

STANDING ON THEIR HIND LEGS TO SAY,
"HELLO," AS PEOPLE WALK BY, HOPING
THEY WILL THROW THEM A NUT OR TWO,

IF THEY DO, THE SQUIRRELS TAKE IT AND
RUN, WHILE SAYING, "TOOT-A-LOO, AND
THANK YOU FOR MY NUT STEW," AS THEY
RUN UP THE TREE, CARE FREE, INTO THE
HOLEOF THE THEIR HOME.

This poem was inspired by a scene while looking out of
my window in the living room during the fall.

MONTH OF JUNE

SAY, IS IT JUNE ALREADY?

THE SWEET NECTURE OF

FLOWERS HAVE BLOOMED,

JUNE IS KNOWN FOR
MANY BRIDES AND GROOMS,

WEDDINGS TO BE PERFORMED

AND MANY BABIES
BORN……………..

VACATIONS ARE
PLANNED,

TO RELAX AND BE
GRAND……….…..

SOON JULY WILL
FOLLOW RIGHT AFTER TO
TAKE ITS PLACE

WITH FUN AND
LAUGHTER AND MANY
THINGS AFTER

There is something about the month of
June besides the official start of summer.
It seems that everything happens from
weddings to vacations and cookouts.

36

THE GOLDEN FLOWER

A SIDE PETAL OF ONE
LITTLE FLOWER

DISPLAYS ITS
UNIQUENESS WITHOUT
A FLAW

THE CLOSER I LOOK,
THE MORE I'M AMAZED,

TO GAZE AND BEHOLD
ITS GOLDEN MAZE

LITTLE WHITE FOX

LITTLE WHITE FOX ALL
CUDDLED IN THE SNOW,

STARING TO SEE WHICH
WAY THAT HE SHOULD
GO,

HE CHANGES HIS
MIND AND DECIDES
TO STAY LONGER,
UNTIL HIS APPETITE
BECOMES OF HUNGER

AS HE STARES HE WATCHES
FOR PREY,

WITH HIS SHARP DARK EYES
AND HIS NOSE THAT
LOOK'S OF SPRINKLED
WHEY

This poem was written from the picture of this beautiful white fox. It looks like whey or cream of wheat is on his nose, but of course I know it is snow.

LAZY LITTLE SEAL

LAZY LITTLE SEAL

DON'T YOU WANT TO PLAY

AND WADDLE WITH THE OTHERS

WHILE IT'S STILL DAY

I like this picture because it looks like the seal is being lazy as if he is looking at the other seals playing and thinking in his mind to go ahead because he doesn't feel like it, and to have enough fun for him too. That is how this poem birthed.

THANK YOU FOR SOWING A SEED

THANK YOU FOR BEING A FRIEND IN A TIME OF NEED

IT'S OBVIOUS YOUR HEART IS UNSELFISH AND NOT OF GREED

YOU CAN REST TO SURE THAT THE PLANTING OF YOUR SEED

WILL RETURN LIKE A BEAUTIFUL FLOWER

FOR THE TORAH OF YAH SAYS WHEN YOU GIVE IN SECRET

HE WILL REWARD YOU IN THE OPEN

I chose this background because the picture displays a healthy flower planted in healthy soil. The flowers look very healthy, therefore the seed was placed in good soil before placing it in this soil. There was a time I was in need of some help and the person that helped me did a good thing because it was a spare of moment situation. The word of Yah says that when one gives in secret he will reward that person in the open. What she did for me I have done so many times for others, so the seed I sowed was returned back to me. There are many people that like to show off in the open when they do things for people, and scripture says that they have already had their reward because of them wanting to impress people and get the praises of men. When I am a blessing to people I like to do it in private like the scripture speaks about and it is always returned. I hate when people call themselves being a blessing to me but are loud announcing what they are doing, for others to see. To do that is not of scripture and it is really about wanting to be impressive in others eyes. But in the eyes of Yahuah it is not impressive at all.

LIVING ROOM

A LIVING ROOM IS LIKE A
ROOM OF COMFORT

YOU CAN LOUNGE IN YOUR
PJ'S OR A GOWN

JUST HANGING AROUND
WHATEVER YOU WEAR,

JUST BE COMFORTABLE
BECAUSE YOU
MAKE YOUR HOME.......

SO MAKE IT TO BE
WHAT COMFORTS YOU

This poem is an opinion of what I think a living
room is used for outside of entertaining guest

APPRECIATION

THIS IS A TOKEN TO SHOW MY APPRECIATION

THAT WHAT YOU GAVE FROM THE HEART IS NOT IN VAIN;

DURING THE TIME YOU WERE SUFFERING

EMOTIONAL PAIN,

YOU STILL TOOK THE TIME TO GIVE TO ME,

ALTHOUGH YOU WERE DRAINED,

NOW I WANT TO THANK YOU FROM MY HEART

FOR THINKING OF ME RIGHT FROM THE START

This poem was written for a former Director I use to work with.
During that time she was suffering from cancer and still took
the time out to give gifts to her staff. I just thought that it was a
very unselfish act and I was very touched by it. So I wrote this
poem and gave her a gift as well.